MW00760399

"The best way to conduct a successful negotiation is for all parties to be satisfied when you conclude the agreement."

"Negotiating is not a competitive sport."

Negotiate Your Way to Success

24 Steps to Building Agreement

STEVEN P. COHEN

McGraw-Hill

New York   Chicago   San Francisco   Lisbon
London   Madrid   Mexico City   Milan   New Delhi
San Juan   Seoul   Singapore   Sydney   Toronto

The **McGraw·Hill** Companies

Copyright © 2007 by McGraw-Hill, Inc. All rights reserved. Printed in the United States of America. Except as permitted under the United States Copyright Act of 1976, no part of this publication may be reproduced or distributed in any form or by any means, or stored in a data base or retrieval system, without prior written permission of the publisher.

4 5 6 7 8 9 0   DOC/DOC   1 5

ISBN-13: 978-0-07-149832-6
ISBN-10: 0-07-149832-X

This publication is designed to provide accurate and authoritative information in regard to the subject matter covered. It is sold with the understanding that the publisher is not engaged in rendering legal, accounting, or other professional service. If legal advice or other expert assistance is required, the services of a competent professional person should be sought.

—From a Declaration of Principles Jointly Adopted by a
Committee of the American Bar Association and a
Committee of Publishers and Associations

McGraw-Hill books are available at special discounts to use as premiums and sales promotions, or for use in corporate training programs. For more information, please write to the Director of Special Sales, Professional Publishing, McGraw-Hill, Two Penn Plaza, New York, NY 10121-2298. Or contact your local bookstore.

This book is printed on acid-free paper.

Library of Congress Cataloging-in-Publication Data

Cohen, Steven P.
Negotiate your way to success : 24 steps to building agreement / Steven P. Cohen.
    p. cm.
Includes bibliographical references and index.
ISBN-13: 978-0-07-149832-6 (paperba ck : alk. paper)
ISBN-10: 0-07-149832-X (alk. paper)
1. Negotiation in business. I. Title.
HD58.6.C627 2007
658.4'052—dc22

2007013937

To order
Negotiate Your
Way to Success
call 1-800-842-3075

Contents

☑ *Negotiation success*

*T*his book has three aims: to help you become good at negotiating, increase your confidence, and improve the rewards you get from concluding an effective negotiation.

The focus of these 24 lessons is on negotiating in business; negotiating effectively can benefit you in various ways in your career. But these lessons also can help you negotiate more effectively in any area of your life.

Negotiation is a universal human activity: We all engage in bargaining and making deals with the people around us more often than we realize. All of us need good negotiation skills in our business activities but will find that these skills are also valuable in our personal lives.

Several years ago, after I had conducted our flagship negotiation course, I sent out to the course participants a follow-up form to elicit long-term evaluations. One participant responded that he had not used negotiation in his professional life—but he had used it to save his marriage.

I hope this book will help you improve your professional skills as a negotiator. I assume that's why you are reading it. But I feel sure that you also can use what you learn from this book to negotiate for personal matters, and the additional benefits for you personally can be very significant.

These lessons present negotiation paradigms and philosophical underpinnings so that you can get a better understanding of the purposes for the specific tools and techniques that are recommended here. These lessons define and explain terms and concepts that you already understand, such as "interests" and "positions," but that you should understand differently so that you can negotiate better. The final five lessons bring all of the preceding 19 lessons together, focusing on the negotiation process and summarizing what I call the seven essentials of the wisdom of negotiating.

You'll find that these lessons do not promulgate hard-and-fast rights and wrongs. Effective negotiators know that each negotiation is unique and that being flexible can make the difference between producing positive results and wasting time. This book emphasizes the idea that you should not view negotiation as a competition exercise and that the best way to conduct a successful negotiation is for all the parties to be satisfied when the agreement has been concluded.

"When I told my father I planned to train people how to negotiate and mentioned that many people feel the need to become more confident, he was dumbfounded: 'Don't people know negotiating is fun?'"

☑ *Understand negotiation*

Sometimes people find themselves in situations in which they want or need to make a decision or a deal with others. Unless they all agree immediately on every point, there is a need for a mutually acceptable process. Negotiation is one name for various joint decision-making processes.

Negotiation succeeds when the parties reach an agreement that they feel mutually committed to fulfilling. Fairness is crucial to effective negotiation. A party who feels that he or she has been treated unfairly may be unwilling to keep an agreement. People who try to take advantage of others are taking risks. Negotiation calls for contributions from all parties so that the agreement is shared and durable.

It is not negotiation if your boss gives you an order that you must obey. It is not negotiation if an outsider arbitrates a conflict and the parties are legally bound by the arbitrator's decision. It is not negotiation if the parties are not working to reach an agreement together.

Negotiation can be either *confrontational* or *cooperative.*

People with a confrontational approach want to win as much as possible. This is shortsighted: They may win, but other parties are unlikely to want to deal with them again.

People with a cooperative approach understand that negotiation is a way to benefit all the parties. They build long-term, mutually beneficial relationships.

Cooperative, *interest-based* negotiation is particularly effective among people who are different culturally, ethnically, or economically. It is necessary to focus on interests instead of differences, which can create obstacles to agreement.

Negotiation is not a competitive sport. Each party should pursue his or her own interests, but the goal is not to crush the other parties. The goal is for all the parties to do the best they can for themselves.

Effective negotiation is a process in which parties pursue their interests to reach an agreement that meets as many of those interests as possible. If the parties are not satisfied with the process as well as the results, they are less likely to fulfill the promises in the agreement.

It is important to understand the following three basic concepts of negotiation:

Know that negotiation is a joint decision-making process: A negotiation is successful when all the parties end up committed to fulfilling the agreement. Fairness is crucial.

Know what negotiation is not: It is not an order imposed by someone in authority. It is not a decision made by an arbitrator. It is not a competition to defeat and even destroy the other party.

Know that negotiation can be either confrontational or cooperative: It is confrontational to want to win every point. It is cooperative to negotiate so that all the stakeholders win. This is interest-based negotiation.

"Negotiating is not a competitive sport."

✓ *Focus on interests*

*D*istinguishing between *interests* and *positions* is critical to understanding negotiation. A position is *what we want.* An interest is *why we want what we want.* Therefore, ask questions such as "How will that approach do what you want?" and "If we agree to that, what goal will you achieve?"

Taking a position usually limits your ability to bargain by reducing your choices. It is smarter to know your interests and pursue them. If you focus on the benefits you expect from negotiating rather than on a specific outcome and if you keep an open mind, you're likely to discover other outcomes that would work for you. When all the parties focus on interests, not on positions, they are more flexible and can reach an agreement that will work.

Once you know your interests, prioritize them. Then you can determine how committed you must be to each of them.

Generally, there are *fundamental* or *primary* interests—what you must have—and *derivative* or *secondary* interests—what will enable you to pursue your primary interests. Sometimes we must deal with derivative interests first so that we then can deal with fundamental interests. Prioritize your interests to decide what steps to take and in what order and to develop strategies.

When you are negotiating, focus on your own interests first. Also consider the interests of your stakeholders: the company, the members of your work team, your family. Which are primary? Which are secondary? How should those interests influence your negotiating?

Consider the interests of the other parties as well. The better you know their interests, the more effectively you can negotiate. Similarly, try to learn about the interests of their stakeholders, which may influence their negotiating.

Keep the following three points in mind:

Know your interests, not just your position: Why do you want what you want? Prioritize your interests. Which ones are fundamental? Which ones are derivative? How committed must you be to each of them?

Know what others want and need: Understand the interests of your constituents, the other parties, and those parties' constituencies. Ask questions. More important, pay attention to the answers.

Deal with positional bargainers carefully: If someone makes an unacceptable proposal, say nothing and show no emotion. If someone shouts or uses strong language, let it go. If someone can't accept any alternatives, try to learn what interests underlie that person's position. If someone acts like a bully, say, "I am afraid we may fail to reach agreement." Fear of failing may end the bullying.

> *"If you take the positional approach and make every item on your list of wants equally important, it will be more difficult to get what you want or to figure out on which items you might be able to compromise."*

☐ Use the fourth C: confront

☑ Use the three C's

*P*eople often believe that the objective of interest-based negotiation is to reach agreement on *common* interests: Each party wants the same results for the same reasons. That is certainly possible, but more often the parties reach agreement by addressing interests that are *complementary*: The parties want the same result, but because it will serve different interests.

The third type of interests is *conflicting*—when the parties' interests are in opposition.

They have nothing in common, and it seems there are no complementary interests that will make it easy to reach an agreement.

In that situation, the parties must determine whether to negotiate or to look elsewhere for solutions. There may be no realistic alternative. When that happens, it is best to break down the issues under consideration into smaller points or use questioning and listening to build relationships to help reduce the chance of conflict.

If you must try to reach agreement when interests conflict, build the possibility of agreement. Look for small things about which the parties can agree: the time and place to meet, the items to put on the agenda and the order for discussing them, even shared interests in areas such as sports, politics, and food.

Then examine the issues to be resolved and look for small elements about which the parties do not disagree. It can be helpful to spend time agreeing on language to describe the problem, points of less importance, or short-term fixes to minor elements of the problem.

Such efforts can lower the emotional level of the conflict and help the parties communicate.

These three points about the three C's are key:

Understand the three C's: Don't focus on the *conflicting* interests—when the parties' interests are in opposition. Don't expect to reach agreement on *common* interests—when the parties want the same results for the same reasons. It's generally most effective to negotiate through *complementary* interests: The parties want the same result, but it will serve different interests.

Build confidence: Parties in conflict can negotiate more effectively when they can develop confidence in each other and feel that they can work together in a collaborative, cooperative way to reach an agreement.

Consider compromise as a last resort: Compromise is a mechanism for meeting in the middle, requiring each party to yield on his or her objectives. Compromise is usually most effective when the parties are at odds over the same thing. Then it's often logical to split the difference that separates them.

"In the Tao Te Ching, Lao Tzu tells us, 'The journey of 1000 miles begins with the first step.' This observation can help us reduce the barrier of conflicting interests that may make agreement seem impossible. Unless we start, we cannot finish."

—The Three C's of Interest. Copyright © 2001 Steven P. Cohen. All rights reserved.

✔ *Know whether to leave*

*Y*ou negotiate to get something better than what you can get without negotiating: your *best alternative to a negotiated agreement* (BATNA). If you can do better through negotiating, negotiate. If you can't, don't.

Before negotiating, understand your ability to achieve your objectives on your own or with others. What resources can you influence or control? What resources can other parties bring to the table?

In all negotiations, the BATNAs of the parties are a measure of the balance of power. Each party needs the others in some way. In preparing, develop a sense of all the BATNAs.

How can you strengthen your BATNA? How can you weaken the BATNAs of the other parties? You want to promote your interests but not work against the interests of other parties and reduce their opportunity to gain from negotiating—and their incentive to negotiate.

What do you know about the topics of the negotiation? What experience do you have with the other parties? What do your colleagues know? What assumptions are you making? Can you justify them? How confident do you feel? What factors may arise during the negotiation that could change your BATNA? Which factors will be most influential with the other parties? What are their interests? What should you reveal? What may not matter to the other parties?

Information is the fundamental asset in negotiation. Keep gathering information. Keep assessing your situation.

Be alert to changes in your BATNA and the others' BATNAs. The better you understand all the BATNAs and deal with the changes, the better able you will be to work toward an agreement.

The BATNAs in a negotiation do not determine the outcome. Other factors also matter, such as creativity, commitment to a particular outcome, and concern about a long-term relationship. Knowing your choices at all times can help you overcome an unfavorable power balance.

Keep track of your BATNA. Are you making progress or wasting time? Be alert to signals that negotiation is not working for you.

Know your BATNA: It tells you whether negotiating is worth the effort. Be aware of changes in your BATNA.

Work with all the BATNAs: Try to strengthen your BATNA and weaken the other BATNAs. The better you understand them, the better you can judge whether it is in your interest to continue negotiating or to walk away.

Be ready to walk: Knowing when it's wise to leave a negotiation can make the process work far better for you. If nothing changes your BATNA, negotiation may not be worth the time.

"The balance of power . . . does not determine the outcome of the negotiation. Examining choices . . . , both before and during the negotiation process, can help you overcome an unfavorable power balance."

☐ Put your faith in fate

☑ *Inoculate yourself*

*I*noculation is the process of preparing for negotiation so that you can commit to your strategies, objectives, and interests. Inoculation can protect you against surprises, help you avoid saying something wrong, and reassure you about your objectives and your ways of achieving them. Inoculation includes the issues to be discussed and the relationships of the parties and their history so that you can avoid making inaccurate assumptions and touching sensitive areas that could distract the parties from the crucial issues.

Study the issues thoroughly; the more you understand, the less likely it is that you will be surprised or stymied by questions.

Choosing among alternatives is critical to negotiation, and so you must know about those alternatives. Inoculate yourself with information ahead of time. Then gather information during the negotiation.

Examine your reasons for pursuing your objectives and the interests underlying those objectives. Are you ready to pursue them? If you have questions, get answers. If you have doubts, find ways to overcome them.

Sometimes the most important inoculation is within our own organization: our business unit, our family, or any other group we depend on to implement an agreement we reach with "outsiders." We need to bring our colleagues into the process before we negotiate to make sure that we can deliver what we intend to offer.

This is particularly important when you negotiate as a representative. Consider the impact of your actions on the stakeholders who will be affected by the negotiation. Be aware of their needs.

As you go through the process of inoculation, you learn more about your BATNA (best alternative to a negotiated agreement). The knowledge you gain may enable you to improve your BATNA even before negotiation begins and to think of ways to weaken the BATNAs of the other parties.

Inoculation can be considered in terms of three C's—competence, conviction, and confidence:

Build your competence: The main purpose of inoculation is to know more. Know the issues of the negotiations, your interests, the interests of the other parties, and other information that is relevant to the context, including the history.

Go forward with conviction: Unless you believe in what you're doing, you can't expect to convince others. If you're not enthusiastic about what you're trying to achieve, you will have difficulty engendering enthusiasm among others. Conviction and enthusiasm are contagious.

Negotiate with confidence: If you have faith in yourself, it makes you more believable and more likely to convince others. Of course, it's best if your confidence is based on competence and conviction.

"What convinces is conviction. Believe in the argument you are advancing. If you don't, you're as good as dead."

—Lyndon B. Johnson

☐ Assume and believe

☑ *Get information*

---

*I*noculation is understanding. The better you understand a situation, the more inoculated you are against surprises and mistakes. Prepare well. It can make all the difference.

Understand the interests underlying your objectives and the interests underlying the objectives of the other parties. Then you can negotiate with greater competence and confidence. You will have a better sense of how to negotiate and how the possible resolutions to the issues will serve your interests. You'll also be less likely to be surprised by the issues that arise.

Work to get a better understanding of the big picture surrounding the negotiation. Find out more about the parties with whom you'll be negotiating. Check with people who know the parties.

Don't conclude that you know everything and are prepared for anything. You may not understand all the factors that are important to other parties, and so you'll probably make assumptions. Test all those assumptions if possible. One way to do that is by using the negotiation to gather information.

Since information is the fundamental asset for negotiation, the better you listen, the better you'll negotiate. Gathering information requires a balance between speaking and listening. You can get the most information by asking open-ended questions and then listening closely and carefully to the answers. Active listening requires paying full attention to others rather than focusing on yourself.

If you listen carefully from the start, you can better understand the issues and why they matter to the parties. You can get a sense of the objectives or interests they are likely to pursue and even how they're likely to do that. Perhaps they will reveal things you may not have considered.

Here are three more suggestions:

Set an example for reciprocity: People aren't always accustomed to having others pay close attention to them. When you make it clear that you have been listening closely, you raise the level of civility in the conversation. The underlying statement you are making is "Okay, I listened to you; now you can listen to me."

Check your understanding: After you've listened to a person, say something like "Then if I understand you correctly, you said A, B, C, and D." Don't repeat everything word for word, but make sure you've understood the other person. It does not mean you agree, of course.

Don't react if you don't agree: Sometimes other parties present ideas with which you simply cannot agree. Then it may be wisest not to react. Use the power of silence. This tactic takes a great deal of self-control, but it enables you to make your point effectively without adding emotion to the discussion.

"Asking a question and ignoring the answer is like searching for buried treasure and then abandoning it once you find it."

☑ *Prepare for the process*

*W*hen you inoculate yourself, it's not just about the subject matter; it also should involve the negotiation process and the items or ideas you plan to discuss.

Part of the preparation can include agreeing on some of the process issues. Those issues may seem simple, but they can influence the dynamics and the outcome significantly.

Where are you meeting? Will one party have a "home field advantage"? When are you meeting? How long will you be meeting? Who is "yielding" on these process issues? Will that yielding create a sense of reciprocity?

What issues should be on the agenda? Which issues are you prepared to discuss? In what order should those issues be addressed? Easier issues first and then work up to the tougher issues? Tougher issues first? Mix easy and tough?

When the parties agree on the agenda in advance, there are advantages. Each learns about the others' priorities. Each can prepare better. Also, in cooperating to develop the agenda, they can become comfortable working together, and so the negotiation may proceed more smoothly.

The better we understand our strengths and weaknesses as deal makers, the more likely it is that what we don't say will underscore what we do say. The inoculation process must include determining our capacity to decide and to act as we negotiate and fulfill the elements of any agreements.

You are not fully inoculated unless you understand your bottom line: the point beyond which you cannot bargain, the limits to any deal you would consider. Understand your bottom line and the way it differs from your BATNA. Then you can negotiate far more intelligently and effectively.

Here are three more aspects of preparation:

Make sure your teammates are on the same page: If you need your teammates—whether work colleagues or family members—to accept and support deals you hope to make, involve them before you negotiate.

Inoculate the other parties: If you have an ongoing relationship with them, inoculation is probably a normal result of your interaction. Negotiations with new parties, however, require inoculation as a part of the preparation. One question you should ask is whether the parties who are negotiating have the authority to make decisions and fulfill any commitments they make.

Prepare for surprise negotiations: We can't inoculate ourselves before every negotiation. Sometimes there is no warning that a negotiation is about to happen. Practicing the discipline of inoculation can be critical to success when we haven't had time to prepare fully.

"Getting into the habit of inoculating yourself before negotiating helps build the instincts you need to negotiate effectively."

☐ **Trust your instincts**

☑ *Know why to prepare*

*O*ne reason to prepare for negotiation is to get a sense of what is going to be important and/or relevant in reaching decisions. Another reason is to develop a map outlining the information you need to uncover during negotiation so that the negotiation can be more effective and efficient.

Preparation also will make you more competent to negotiate on a particular range of issues with a specific set of parties. You will understand your strengths and weaknesses better so that you can remedy your weaknesses and build on your strengths.

Preparation also can make you more credible: The other parties will take what you say more seriously. If it seems that you're not sufficiently informed, it's harder to negotiate effectively.

Knowing that you are prepared will increase your self-confidence. That confidence can be communicated to the other parties. Also, when you feel confident, you're more likely to remain calm. If you have prepared well, you are less likely to be surprised and lose your cool.

Sometimes even the best negotiators get surprised. It may take time to figure out how a surprise affects your interests. You can't plan for every possibility. Nonetheless, anticipating any possibilities that seem likely should prepare you to think on your seat.

You cannot be certain whether any preparation you do will cover all the issues that may arise in a negotiation. But failing to prepare is far more risky than doing your best to be ready. In negotiation, particularly when the goal is a mutually created agreement that the parties will fulfill willingly, good preparation can make a tremendous difference.

Here are three final points as you get ready to prepare:

Don't gamble on your gut: Some people consider themselves natural negotiators. Their instinctive approach may yield favorable results. But even if their instincts are good, preparation would improve the results. Gambling that you will negotiate effectively by going with gut instincts is risky.

Prepare your teammates: Those around you (colleagues or family members) should know what you're trying to achieve. They may have concerns or suggestions. Don't make promises or raise their expectations to an unrealistic level.

Know what you want and why: This is your basic reality. What you want is your objectives or your position. Why you want it is the understanding that will allow you to assess every possibility in terms of your objectives. Without knowing what and why, you can't prepare and can't hope to benefit from negotiation.

"If you have not prepared for negotiation, you may respond without giving adequate thought to what you say. Remember: Fast answers can lead to long consequences."

☐ **Go solo**

☑ *Work with your team*

Negotiations within your organization are often far more important than negotiations with outsiders. You need to know what others in your organization want and need. You need to know what promises you can make. The others are far more likely to be cooperative in fulfilling their obligations if they feel you have considered their concerns in negotiating an agreement.

Don't take your teammates for granted whether they are work colleagues or family members. Pay serious attention to the relevant interests of the people who will be affected by the results of the negotiation. Otherwise, you are risking negative reactions back home.

Another reason for internal negotiations is to achieve buy-in. Getting your teammates to feel ownership of the agreement is critical to fulfilling your obligations.

As you consult with your teammates and others in the organization, you should keep your BATNA in mind. You may be able to strengthen it if you discover resources that you can access. In fact, you may find that you don't need to negotiate or at least can limit the interests that you bring to the table.

If you negotiate without first consulting your colleagues and then bring back an agreement, they may present some obstacles to delivering on what you've agreed to do. Understanding your organization's capacity to deliver on a deal, finding out the importance of particular specifications, or getting a sense of deadlines or pressures in particular areas of your organization can ensure that an agreement that seems great at the negotiating table is just as great when you bring it back home.

As you engage in "insider negotiations," remember to do these three things:

Prioritize and plan: The hardest part of preparation is understanding and prioritizing the interests you are planning to pursue. As you talk with others in the organization, you should be learning more about the interests you are bringing to the negotiation. You may discover other ways in which negotiating can serve your interests.

Build your BATNA: As you negotiate within the organization, you may find that your BATNA is stronger than you thought or weaker than you believed. You may find that you have less reason to push on some points and more reason to push on others.

Test your knowledge: Whenever you discuss your negotiation plans with people in your organization, consider it a reality check. You can just present them with a plan, or you can solicit their input and possibly discover areas where your information is limited or even inaccurate.

"In negotiation, the three most important words are preparation, preparation, preparation."

☐ **Keep it all in your head**

☑ *Map interests*

*A*n Interest Map* is a graphic way to prepare for a negotiation. You can use a large sheet of paper, a flip chart, or a whiteboard.

Begin with the stakeholders: people concerned in some way with the outcome of the negotiation. Write their names across the sheet, spread out, grouping stakeholders who are related in some way. Underline each name and leave enough space under it to write in that person's interests.

Don't worry about the design. Just show the parties and the stakeholders and their interests.

Then figure out how the interests of each stakeholder are interrelated. Determine any connections.

List your assumptions about each stakeholder's interests, particularly relative to the negotiation. Which are fundamental or primary? Which are derivative or secondary? You will refine the list of interests and check your assumptions as the negotiation goes forward.

Draw lines to connect related interests among stakeholders, especially the negotiating parties and their closest stakeholders. These connections will suggest common or complementary interests that may lead toward agreement. Sometimes the connections among related parties must take top priority; in other situations finding connections among stakeholders on different sides of the issue is more important.

*Copyright © 2001 by Steven P. Cohen. All rights reserved.

The first draft of your Interest Map shows what you know or assume about the situation. Check with teammates to find out about their interests and the interests of other stakeholders.

An Interest Map is a tool for organizing your thoughts and gathering information as you prepare and for determining what information you need, what questions to ask, what assumptions to question, what connections you can use in negotiating, and what creative options could help the parties reach agreement.

Here are three tips for using an Interest Map to avoid problems:

Don't have all the answers: Sometimes when a party thinks of "every possible element that may be relevant to the negotiation," he or she presents far too much information to the other parties. This sends the message that they cannot contribute anything. First, that could be wrong; second, that's not negotiating.

Be prepared for hot buttons: As you prepare your Interest Map, research any issues that could generate emotional reactions. Focus on the issues to be negotiated and try to avoid sensitive issues.

Rule your emotions: It is crucial in negotiating not to let your emotions govern your behavior. If you've prepared appropriately, you should have a good sense of what to expect and minimize the possibility of surprises.

"An Interest Map shows the stakeholders, your best assumptions of their interests, and any connections among the interests of different stakeholders, including the negotiating parties."

☐ Talk, talk, talk

☑ *Ask and listen*

*I*f you've prepared thoroughly, you've mapped the stakeholders' interests and priorities and the possible connections among those interests. You've also made assumptions and possibly discovered gaps in your information. The Interest Map shows what you need to find out about the other parties.

Information is the fundamental asset in negotiation. You want more. You want to check your assumptions and fill in the gaps. You can't learn more by telling what you know. You must listen.

Following are the five basic principles of active listening:

- Pay attention.
- Integrate the information.
- Ask open questions.
- Listen to the answers.
- Verify your understanding.

Pay attention to the other parties. What points or words seem most important? What do their facial expressions and body language express? What emotions are in their words?

Integrate the information you get into the big picture represented on your Interest Map. What can help you develop an agreement?

Ask open questions: the kind that elicits explanations or invites detailed responses. Avoid closed questions (the type that can only be answered with "yes" or "no"). If an answer tells what the party wants, follow up with questions to elicit the underlying interest.

Listen to the answers and listen attentively. The other person should feel and know that you're listening.

Verify your understanding. Get confirmation—"Am I correct in my understanding that you said X and Y and Z?"—or clarification—"Could you explain what you meant when you said A and B but not C?" There's a benefit beyond verifying understanding: Sometimes when people hear their words from another person, they adjust a statement to make it more acceptable.

Here are three final points about active listening:

Influence others in both ways: You can influence others by speaking and writing. But good communication goes in at least two directions. The attention we pay to others also helps us influence them. If you show you're willing to listen to other parties in the negotiation process, that should surprise and impress them.

Take time to listen and then time to think about speaking: Don't try to do both at one time. Often when another party is making a point, we are preparing what we want to say, not listening carefully. You don't need to respond immediately. It's more important to listen attentively.

Create an obligation of reciprocity: This is a secondary reason to check whether you have understood the other person. When you confirm your understanding of what he or she has said, the other person generally feels obligated to listen to you.

"God gave us two ears and one mouth;
we should use them in that ratio."

—Old folk expression

✓ *React strategically*

*A*fter confirming that you understand the other party, say, "Now that I understand you, I would like to think about your ideas before responding to them." That indicates that you have focused attentively and have not been thinking about how to respond.

Shape your response to the other parties' points, sometimes using their words. Show how they have influenced you. This helps you connect with their points and with them.

Make it clear that understanding does not imply agreement. If you disagree with something, say so. If people think you agree and you surprise them later by disagreeing, communication becomes more difficult.

If you consider a proposal unacceptable and your BATNA doesn't let you walk away, the best response may be silence. Reveal nothing in your words or expressions. Your reaction communicates that the other party should try again.

If it's difficult to negotiate with some parties, use the personal information you've gathered about those parties for your Interest Map to connect with them as people.

Ask open-ended questions. That shows interest and respect and keeps people engaged in the negotiation.

If someone presents an idea in a form that seems confusing, problematic, or even unacceptable, rephrase it: "Rather than saying, 'A and B and C,' how would you feel if we said, 'B and A and C'?" You can suggest trying to reflect joint concerns: "How can we rephrase the proposal to make it attractive to more parties?"

If someone seems to be headed away from making progress, don't ask, "What is your point?" Try something like "I'm confused about where you are heading; could you explain your objective more clearly?"

Finally, provide only information that's significant to yourself and the others. Too much information can confuse and possibly frustrate the others and waste time. Of course, never provide information when doing so would be contrary to your interests.

Here are three more suggestions for more effective communication:

Don't lose the points in the words: If someone keeps talking, raising point after point, interrupt politely: "The points you are making are quite interesting. To give each of them appropriate attention, perhaps we should discuss a few at a time."

Keep the playing field level: Negotiation should be characterized by conversational interaction. No party should dominate the conversation. Always be ready to intervene or, if that party is you, stop talking.

Think about the end: Keep asking yourself, "What is the point of this negotiation?" This reminder will help you focus on your interests and your BATNA and avoid wasting time.

"If one party is talking about one thing and another party is talking about something entirely different, you may have a situation that one of my colleagues calls 'Dueling Monologues.'"

☐ Ignore all emotions

☑ *Plan for emotions*

Negotiating can become emotional. Don't let emotions distract you from focusing on interests and reaching an agreement.

Emotions can reveal what makes people tick. What insights can you gain into the other parties' interests, priorities, and problem areas?

As you prepare for negotiation, try to figure out which issues could trigger emotional reactions in any of the parties, including you. Then prepare to deal with those reactions.

If you are surprised by a comment, the way you express that surprise will affect the negotiation. If you've prepared well and anticipated the issues that may arise, you can put the comment in context and focus on meaning rather than emotional impact. When the unexpected happens, think about how it affects your interests and your BATNA.

If someone upsets you, take a moment to consider your choices. You can say very calmly, "If we want to solve the problem, we should consider more closely what we each can gain by working together. If we fail to reach agreement, how will we explain that to our bosses or others?"

If someone says or does something you consider outrageous, use the power of silence, as was recommended earlier in this book. Be careful, though: If you use it too often, it becomes less effective.

If someone expresses frustration or hostility, ask questions and then listen very attentively and obviously. Show that you take the person seriously.

If the negotiation becomes too emotional, try to separate the problem from the people. Give the problem a place of its own. For example, put it on a flip chart. Emphasize collaboration: "Each of us is responsible for dealing with this issue; let's act as a team, with the problem as our common adversary."

Here are three things to avoid so that you can deal with emotions positively:

Don't fear emotions: Plan for them. Emotions can be used to make points that rational arguments can't express. If you know in advance which issues can bring your emotions to the surface, you can plan the time, place, and manner for expressing joy, anger, or stress.

Don't retaliate: It takes a great deal of discipline not to react when you feel attacked. Think about the practical consequences of retaliation. If you remain in control of yourself, you can negotiate far more effectively. Focus on how good it feels not to be losing control of yourself.

Don't accuse: Even if accusations are true, they divide the parties and make negotiation more difficult or even impossible. Focus on common interests.

"Emotions are a legitimate part of negotiation. . . . But if you let your emotions control you, you risk losing control as well as influence over the process."

☐ Do whatever it takes

☑ *Keep it productive*

Many people treat negotiation as an adversarial interaction in which any strategies and tactics are acceptable, but you don't have to be tough to negotiate well. Intimidation generally makes other parties feel resentful and unwilling to fulfill an agreement.

Some negotiators use questions to intimidate. Asking questions is a critical element of negotiation, but presenting a barrage of questions is attacking, not asking. If anyone tries this tactic with you, think hard about how responding would serve your interests.

If a question confuses or bothers you, just ask, "Why are you asking me that?" Maybe you can gain insight into the person's interests and BATNA and shift from interrogation to a more productive interaction.

Be alert for other tactics. Show that you're aware. Take notes: That may stop the use of the other parties' tricks. Ask questions such as "Why did you say that?" and "Why are you doing this?"

If you feel there's a hidden agenda, you can say, "I sense there are important issues that are not being discussed. Is there more I should know about what's happening here?" Show that you're smart and that you expect to be treated with respect.

Don't let offensive words or actions derail a negotiation. If someone says or does something that bothers you, let the person know but don't assume that it was intentional.

One of the biggest challenges in negotiating is to avoid offending. When people feel offended, they may focus less on their interests and negotiating. If something offends you, be frank about it—

without offending. But don't try so hard to be inoffensive that you inhibit your creativity and interaction.

To keep negotiations comfortable and productive, here are three suggestions:

Keep your BATNA in mind: Know when to continue and know when it makes more sense to walk away. Just because you've agreed to negotiate, don't consider yourself obligated to reach an agreement, particularly when others are intentionally making negotiation difficult.

Be proactive: It is not always possible to know what will offend others. It's wise to say something like this early on: "We don't know each other very well. If I say or do anything you find even mildly offensive, please let me know." Then, if that happens, thank the person for being frank.

Provoke with care: It may be a good tactic to provoke someone intentionally. If you do this, be particularly attentive to the reaction. If the person gets angry, apologize quickly and explain your intention. Being open and honest is always a smart policy.

"Through the centuries and from culture to culture, myths have become accepted as the conventional wisdom to describe how to succeed at negotiation."

☐ Jump into the game

☑ *Know how to start*

*A*s you prepare to negotiate, develop realistic expectations. Determine what you expect to gain from negotiating and the limits of what you'll accept.

Know what you can offer and how others value it so that you don't make unrealistic offers. Know your bottom line so that you don't accept unrealistic offers.

In preparing, think about how to put ideas on the table. Should you present the entire proposal all at once? It may make more sense to go step by step, getting reactions at each step. Think about letting others present their ideas first. The more you can learn from them, the better you can present your ideas in ways that are attractive to them.

It may be wise to begin negotiations with confidence-building measures. Working together on logistic issues for the negotiation is one way to build trust and comfort. Others include arriving on time, dressing appropriately, using proper forms of address, engaging in casual conversation, avoiding off-color language or jokes, and finding points in common.

Communication is fundamental to effective negotiation. Unless the parties share an understanding of what they're discussing, they may be agreeing to two or more different interpretations of the same thing. If that happens, they may be reluctant to fulfill the agreement. One of the critical purposes of active listening and verifying is to ensure that all the parties understand something in the same way.

Keep these three things in mind as you enter into a negotiation:

Focus on your interests and instincts: Negotiations don't always take place on a level playing field. Negotiators have different BATNAs, the quality of their preparation will vary, and their negotiation skills generally are different. To negotiate successfully, keep in mind what you want and why and pay attention to your gut feeling.

Win and work the trades: Know the value of every point on the table to you and to the others. Win points early even if they have a lower priority. As the negotiation proceeds, you may be able to trade those wins for points that matter more to you. If you try to win only the points that have a higher priority for you, you may have little or nothing of value to trade.

Distinguish between understanding and agreeing: Make sure others also distinguish between the two. After you verify your understanding of a point, you can add, "Now I understand you correctly, but please don't assume that understanding your point means I agree with it. I disagree with some aspects."

"Develop a clear sense of your bottom line. Once you have established a bottom line, choose how best to use the negotiation process to ensure you will do no worse than that."

☐ Ignore differences

☑ *Work with differences*

***W**e* are surrounded by differences among people. Some seem obvious, such as national and ethnic and linguistic differences. Others are not apparent: differences in perspective and thinking and values, for example.

To negotiate effectively with "outsiders"—from across the industrial park or around the world—you first must negotiate successfully with "insiders." Involve your teammates—coworkers, family members, or whoever—in your preparation. Find out their interests and concerns. Your teammates can help you develop your Interest Map.

Your BATNA—the resources you can control or influence to achieve your objectives—may depend on in-house resources from different "tribes." If that is the case, you should understand how their interests complement yours and how to work together. Find commonalties among the tribes before undertaking external negotiations.

When you are negotiating with people from other cultures, be alert to differences but avoid making assumptions. Try to understand them as individuals. Keep in mind the many ways in which people may differ in negotiating and in dealing with others. Reading can help you prepare, but the best preparation for dealing with cultural differences is an open mind and sensitivity. As always, the more you focus on interests, the better your chance of negotiating wisely and effectively will be.

With people of other cultures (insiders or outsiders), it's crucial to be sensitive to giving or taking offense. Focus on achieving a mutually acceptable agreement. Keep checking your assumptions.

If English is not the first language of all the parties, avoid colloquial expressions and figures of speech. Also, confirm understanding as often as seems necessary.

In negotiating with people of other nationalities and with different legal and cultural norms, make sure that all the parties understand and accept what makes an agreement binding. As in all negotiations, build long-term fulfillment into the agreement. Every negotiation with anyone should include agreeing on incentives and penalties and deciding who determines whether the parties are abiding by the agreement.

Here are three final recommendations for negotiating around cultural differences:

Don't let style distract you from substance: Recognize that cultural differences are simply variations in the art of negotiating. Don't let them keep you from reaching agreement on the issues.

Focus on content: Language is a tool; don't let it become an issue. Whether a party is not a native speaker of your language or simply misuses or mispronounces words, ignore the mistakes unless they affect communication.

Collaborate, don't convert: People often feel tempted to try to convert others to their way of thinking and acting. Sometimes the greater the differences, the greater the temptation. Negotiation is a process for exchanging things of value in a civilized manner. That means respecting differences.

"A negotiator's central obligation is to keep focused on interests, comprehending his or her own and developing an understanding of the other parties' interests. . . . An old friend of mine used to say, 'Don't get hung up on style.'"

☐ Think "money"

☑ *Negotiate on value*

Sometimes negotiators think simply and focus on money. Unfortunately, focusing on money makes negotiators less flexible and creative.

Money is a means of measuring worth that everyone understands. If one thinks in money terms, the least complex way to reach agreement may be compromise. But compromise is often not the best resolution.

If you look only at the "price tag" of any item in a negotiation, you may lose sight of the fact that negotiation is about *value*. And you must understand—and remember—that value is relative: It varies with the situation and the perspective.

In any negotiation, it is important to try to reach a resolution in which every party gains as much value as possible. The key is to find out how much each other party values each element on the table.

If you use your Interest Map, you should find ways in which the parties and their stakeholders would value things on the table in terms of their interests: ego, reputation, desire for control, or whatever. If you think "beyond the money," you can negotiate according to values and probably come up with ways to make an agreement that will satisfy the parties more than will be the case if the agreement is based on money.

Here's a simple example. What's loaf of bread worth? The price tag says $2. But I'm starving, so I value it more than that. You just ate dinner, and so you value it considerably less. Ellie is allergic to wheat, and so it has no value to her. Randy wants to make a sandwich, and so he wants just two slices. If we think of the bread as being worth $2, we probably will seek a compromise: Each of us gets a quarter. How do we each feel about our share?

Keep these three things in mind when negotiating:

Be creative if possible; compromise if necessary: There are two definitions of *compromise*. All parties leave the table equally happy, and all parties leave equally dissatisfied.

Do not confuse price and value: Price is what you pay; *value* is what you receive. In negotiations, price is worth in money and value is worth in terms of situation and perspective.

Find value—don't fake it: You walk a very fine line when you create value in a negotiation. If you exaggerate the value of things on the table to contrive an agreement that's better for yourself, you can lose your credibility: The other parties will trust you less. Don't inflate to manipulate.

"The bigger the pie, the more there is to share."

—Old folk saying

☐ Show off

☑ *Show respect*

*T*o make negotiation work, it is necessary to treat others with respect. There are several ways to show respect at the negotiating table.

One way is to understand how people value something that has been put on the table. This is a reasonably simple sign of respect, part of allowing the others to contribute to developing an agreement. It's also wise. It is even wiser to learn from them than to assume by yourself. And it's a most pragmatic way of encouraging them to buy into the process and the agreement that results.

It's easier to treat the other parties with respect, especially if things get uncomfortable, if you separate the people from the problem. Interest-based negotiation focuses on interests rather than on the parties whose interests they may be. It's not about banging heads but about putting heads together to work out an agreement that addresses all interests.

People usually feel more comfortable negotiating when there's a spirit of sharing, when all are contributing toward a resolution. Don't dominate the action. Try to strike a reasonable balance between your ego and your other interests in a negotiation. Effective negotiators are more interested in bringing about resolution than in being the hero of the game.

Another way to show respect is by caring about confirming mutual understanding. This is particularly important when negotiations get creative. Throughout the negotiation, find gentle ways to ascertain whether the point you've made is clear. And when others make points, check to make sure you understand them.

Mutual understanding is critical. Also, keeping track of understanding as the negotiation progresses is a good way to ensure real buy-in on each element of the deal.

Here are three ways to improve negotiations:

Remember that negotiation is not a competitive sport: Focus on your interests and the interests of your stakeholders. If you try to run the show, the benefit for your ego may not outweigh the harm you do to the process. All the parties should contribute to developing an agreement.

Test your assumptions: Ask questions and use your ears and eyes. Listen for points they repeat. Notice issues that cause them to speak more loudly or with greater intensity. Find out how highly other parties value things on the table and why.

Don't be positional: If you have all the answers, there's no reason for negotiation. Your message to other parties is basically "You don't have anything to contribute to this decision." As with so many things in life, it's not just about the destination but also about the journey.

"Remember that negotiation is a process for deriving benefits from working collaboratively. Don't try to impose on other parties your valuations of elements on the table."

☑ *Think creatively*

*U*sing a creative approach to negotiation can result in solutions that address more interests. Here are three possibilities:

- **Brainstorm.** Write all the ideas on flip charts or whiteboards. After all the parties have stopped contributing, the group can begin to choose the best ideas and make them even better.
- **Have all the parties sit on the same side of the table.** This arrangement underscores the value of collaboration, of joining forces to pursue the interests of all.
- **Use the one-text approach.** Take the thoughts of each party into account and then prepare a single document that outlines a possible resolution. Give each party a chance to comment on the document or revise it. Sharing success can build buy-in and commitment—and a durable agreement.

Your Interest Map provides you with assumptions to check as you search for common ground on which to build an agreement. The map is also a good way to think creatively from the start. It encourages you to find possible interests and connections. The creativity you put into your Interest Map can lead to more creativity in negotiating and inspire other parties to be creative.

If your negotiation strategy contains creative elements such as new ways to solve problems or overcome distrust, a cautious approach makes sense. You and the other negotiators should head in two directions:

- Commit to the big picture by agreeing that you want to agree.

- Examine all the ideas one by one to weed out potential deal breakers.

When you propose a creative package, be careful to offer it as an overall menu rather than a take-it-or-leave-it positional proposal.

Here are three more suggestions for being a more creative negotiator:

Expand the possibilities: Open your mind to thinking outside the box both in preparing and in negotiating. How likely is it that you'll sit down at the table with a plan that all the parties will accept?

Encourage collaboration: The way you respond to contributions from others either encourages collaboration or discourages it. The phrase "win/win" is overused, but unless parties feel they have gained from negotiating, you can't expect to make a deal. Even if you form the perfect plan in advance, they may not like it if they don't contribute to it.

Give people time . . . and freedom: When you get creative in a negotiation, don't be surprised if the other parties need to consider the ideas one by one. Don't expect them to understand and accept your ideas immediately and totally. That's not negotiating.

"Prepare with an open mind. Good preparation is a crucial first step in bringing creativity into the process. An open mind to what others contribute can bring it all together."

✓ *Develop the agenda*

*T*he agenda is central to planning for negotiation. The items scheduled and the order can affect the outcome of a negotiation significantly.

From your preparation, you should have a good idea of the issues to discuss in line with your interests and what you assume to be the interests of the other parties. Consider the relative importance of each item on the agenda and the potential strategic consequences of the order of those items.

If the negotiating parties are working together to develop the agenda, they are building a spirit of collaboration and agreement from the start. Also, each party then knows what the other parties want to discuss or avoid discussing.

Make sure that the agenda offers you an opportunity to do better than your BATNA. If it does not, why waste your time negotiating with parties who have such a different view of what's important?

Each party should come to the table with a copy of the agenda. That makes it more likely that all the parties will have a sense of the big picture. It can be frustrating to deal with parties whose focus is so narrow that they are obstructing the progress of the negotiation.

The written agenda can form a record of the progress of the negotiation. The group can summarize any agreement reached on each agenda item even if the details of those agreements are to be developed later. Copies of the agenda with summaries should be given to the parties at the end of the session. That keeps them all on the same page, literally.

Here are three more points about agendas:

Learn to prioritize and order: A negotiation may come up suddenly when you bump into someone or answer the phone. You will not always have an agenda in mind. The practice of organizing agendas when you have time to plan will help you learn to improvise agendas.

Trust but be wary: Be alert to any party trying to delete an item from the agenda or add an item to it. If all the parties agree to the deletion or addition, that's good. But if any of the parties disagree with the addition or deletion and the "change agent" insists on the modification, this may be a sign of bad faith that reduces confidence in the long-term credibility of that party.

Prevent memory loss: If a negotiation continues beyond a single meeting, all the parties should initial a copy of the summarized elements of the agreement. Then nobody can say, "I don't remember discussing that."

"Keep in mind that every negotiation is different and that negotiations don't always follow the same script."

☐ Try "take it or leave it"

☑ *Bargain "if . . . then . . . "*

---

*B*argaining. For many people that term suggests pushing and haggling. In a fair negotiation process it means making connections among interests and suggesting exchanges of things of value.

You could aim at getting the best deal, no matter what. But if you treat negotiating as a competitive sport, people may be unwilling to keep any agreement they make with you or to deal with you at all.

You need to determine when bargaining is likely to yield better results. Your BATNA should give you a sense of the value of bargaining.

How should you bargain?

If you present a take-it-or-leave-it position, you lose flexibility and freedom.

You're far more likely to negotiate effectively if you present an offer with an incentive. Listen carefully to the other parties. Get a better sense of their interests and priorities. When you know what they want and why, you will be more able to make offers that should appeal to them.

One effective way to offer a bargain is to present it as an "if ... then ..." exchange: "If you promise to do this for me, then I will do that for you." Presenting an offer in this way shows how a bargain benefits the parties.

Making the trading process transparent can make the parties more confident about the value of the deal and about being able to depend on each other.

When you use the "if ... then ..." approach, there is clear communication among the parties; everyone is on the same page, at least for that element of the negotiation.

Here are three suggestions about using your Interest Map to chart bargaining routes:

Keep your Interest Map in hand or in mind: You may decide to bring your Interest Map to the table. That way you can check it and take notes on it. If you do not have it in hand, keep the information and the questions it raises in mind.

Use your Interest Map to connect: You can communicate better at the table by listening than by talking. And what you learn through listening can help you talk more effectively. Your Interest Map shows what you know and what questions you need to ask. Use it to gain information and connect with the other parties.

Soften the impact of surprises: At the table a party may surprise you—intentionally or not. If something arises that surprises, check your Interest Map. Does it show anything that would enable you to respond better to the surprise?

"Information is the fundamental asset in negotiation."

☐ Just get an agreement

✓ *Build commitment*

A crucial part of most negotiations is creating an agreement that will work. In preparing to negotiate, think about whatever could go wrong with an agreement. Keep those concerns in mind when you negotiate.

What can go wrong? There are many answers to that question. The following list can help you start listing potential problems for your specific situation.

- The party doesn't have the authority to bind his or her company.
- A strike, a fire in a factory, or another unexpected event keeps a party from delivering.
- The product does not meet specifications.
- Needs or resources change.
- A party is hit by a lawsuit and has difficulty getting financing to deliver as specified.
- Attorneys representing one or more parties become an obstacle to the agreement.

How can you feel confident that the other parties will fulfill whatever agreement you reach? Start by asking yourself, "What's the worst that can happen?" The answers will help the parties develop ways to feel more confident that an agreement will work for all of them.

Use this worst-case analysis to determine ways to ensure that the parties will fulfill the agreement. Then, while negotiating the agreement, develop means of measuring performance and enforcing the agreement.

In addition to taking the preventive approach while you are negotiating, consider what mechanisms you and the other parties should have in place during the term of the agreement.

Ask yourself, "How can I be sure X is fulfilling his or her part of the bargain? Are there things he or she needs to do to monitor my performance?"

Here are three suggestions for building commitment into an agreement:

Establish objective, measurable criteria: How will you define performance? This should be done in such a way that a third party such as an arbitrator or a judge could make a determination if necessary. Some trade associations set standards for evaluating performance. You also could consult an independent source of expertise.

Consider going outside: It may make sense to find a disinterested third party to monitor the performance of the parties. An objective outsider may be more credible to the parties when it comes to determining whether their performance measures up to their promises.

Choose incentives over penalties: Some agreements contain penalties for performance problems. Unfortunately, the burden is on the wronged party to assess the penalty, adding inconvenience to injury. As an alternative, many agreements contain incentives for appropriate performance. It may be wise to have the negotiation include decisions on incentives.

"In all negotiations, build long-term fulfillment into the agreement. Agreeing on incentives and penalties and deciding who determines whether the parties are keeping their side belongs in every negotiation process."

☑ *Negotiate smart*

Come to the table with aggressive but realistic expectations. Set them carefully: When you negotiate, you are not likely to exceed your expectations.

You will do better in the give-and-take of negotiation if your expectations are aimed high enough to give you room for concessions. Plan for what you are willing to concede or trade away in order to serve your interests.

Compromise is not a necessary element of a negotiated agreement. Compromise may work well if the negotiation is about a single issue or a very small range of issues, but if the negotiation is complex, compromise may be extraordinarily difficult.

Compromise may be the best answer when reaching agreement is a goal in itself. However, in interest-based negotiation, reaching agreement may be less valuable than protecting what you already have: your BATNA. Is reaching agreement more important than what you must concede in compromising?

Throughout the negotiation process, think about the interrelations among issues and strategies. Your preparation should make you aware of issues that may arise. Understanding how each decision may affect others will help you negotiate more effectively. Understanding the priority of each agenda item helps you keep it in context so that you negotiate more efficiently.

Finally, how do you know when a negotiation is complete?

The parties need to agree on some way of signifying closure: a handshake, a press release, or an elaborate contract.

Under contract law, an agreement can be changed if its parties agree to the changes, but unilateral changes cannot be binding on all the parties. If circumstances change, you can contact the other parties and suggest changing the agreement. If they agree, do it. If they do not, consider the legal and business consequences that can result if the agreement is broken.

Follow these three suggestions to survive and succeed:

Think ahead: The most successful negotiators are like top chess players. They are thinking beyond the immediate move or even the next move, thinking about how the results of those moves will influence subsequent moves in the negotiation process.

Sweat the small stuff: If you think that something is a small detail, don't let it go by saying, "We'll cross that bridge if we come to it." The small stuff you ignore during a negotiation can grow suddenly into big stuff.

Take breaks: Negotiating right can be overwhelming. You can risk overload that can cause problems. Take a time-out if you need a break. Even a trip to the bathroom can help. It may be smart to schedule breaks.

"Negotiation is not rocket science. Everyone—even children too young to read this book—has a negotiation style. There are always choices to make. There is no consistently right formula."

☑ *Build with seven pillars*

*T*he Seven Pillars of Negotiational Wisdom* are the vital elements of the negotiation process. You must prioritize among them each time you negotiate.

1. **Relationship.** If you negotiate with certain people time after time, it's smart to consider gains or losses in terms of ongoing relationships. The value of the relationships can have a significant impact on the way you negotiate.

2. **Interests.** In interest-based negotiation, each party works toward the agreement most favorable to his or her interests. Focus on all the interests at the table to develop a better result than you could achieve without negotiating.

3. **BATNA.** If you understand your BATNA, you have a good idea whether it's worth negotiating and with whom. In preparing, investigate resources you control or influence that can serve your interests. What information do you need to decide whether negotiation will strengthen or weaken your BATNA?

4. **Creativity.** While preparing and while negotiating, consider how a creative approach could serve the interests of all the parties. With positional or adversarial negotiators, creativity may become the top priority.

*Copyright © 2000 by Steven P. Cohen. All rights reserved.

5. **Fairness.** The parties must consider the negotiation process fair or they may feel less committed to an agreement. If your priority is to reach an agreement, be sensitive to perceptions of your behavior and fairness.

6. **Commitment.** A negotiation is successful only when it yields an agreement to which the parties are committed. The parties should feel good about the process and motivated to make the agreement work.

7. **Communication.** Information is the fundamental asset in negotiation, and communication is the way information moves from one party to others. Your Interest Map shows what you know and what you need to know to work with all the interests at the table.

Foundation of the Seven Pillars: Preparation

The seven pillars are supported by one foundation: *preparation.*

Here are three more points about the seven pillars:

Don't let the forest obscure the trees: Negotiating can be overwhelming. Pay attention to the seven pillars and the foundation. Then it should be easier to negotiate and you should be more effective.

Bring creativity into the process: If you think about the process as well as the proposals, you may be able to contribute more creatively. Try to think about the situation from a different perspective.

Judge your fairness from the outside: Is the negotiation process fair? Are you being fair? How you would feel if your behavior or the result of the process were reported in your local newspaper or assessed by your mother?

> *"While the importance of each of the Seven Pillars may vary from negotiation to negotiation, it is crucial to remember that the Seven Pillars are supported by one foundation: preparation."*

"Information is the fundamental asset in negotiation. Keep gathering information."

The McGraw-Hill
Professional Education Series

How to Manage Performance: 24 Lessons for Improving Performance
By Robert Bacal (0-07-143531-X)

Goal-focused, commonsense techniques for stimulating greater productivity in the workplace and fostering true commitment.

Dealing with Difficult People: 24 Lessons for Bringing Out the Best in Everyone
By Rick Brinkman and Rick Kirschner (0-07-141641-2)

Learn about the 10 types of problem people and how to effectively respond to them to improve communication and collaboration.

How to Motivate Every Employee: 24 Proven Tactics to Spark Productivity in the Workplace
By Anne Bruce (0-07-141333-2)

By a master motivator and speaker, this book quickly reviews practical ways you can turn on employees and enhance their performance and your own.

Six Sigma for Managers: 24 Lessons to Understand and Apply Six Sigma Principles in Any Organization
By Greg Brue (0-07-145548-5)

Introduces the fundamental concepts of Six Sigma and details practical steps to spearhead a Six Sigma program in the workplace.

How To Be a Great Coach: 24 Lessons for Turning on the Productivity of Every Employee
By Marshall J. Cook (0-07-143529-8)

Today's most effective coaching methods to dramatically improve the performance of your employees.

Leadership When the Heat's On: 24 Lessons in High Performance Management
By Danny Cox and John Hoover (0-07-141406-1)

Learn hands-on techniques for infusing any company with results-driven leadership at every level, especially during times of organizational turmoil.

Networking for Career Success: 24 Lessons for Getting to Know the Right People
By Diane Darling (0-07-145603-1)

Learn the steps for making mutually beneficial career connections and the know-how to cultivate those connections for the benefit of everyone involved.

Why Customers Don't Do What You Want Them To: 24 Solutions to Common Selling Problems
By Ferdinand Fournies (0-07-141750-8)

This results-focused guidebook will help you to recognize and resolve 20 common selling problems and objections and help you move beyond them.

The Powell Principles: 24 Lessons from Colin Powell, a Legendary Leader
By Oren Harari (0-07-141109-7)

Colin Powell's success as a leader is universally acknowledged. Quickly learn his approach to leadership and the methods he uses to move people and achieve goals.

Project Management: 24 Lessons to Help You Master Any Project
By Gary Heerkens (0-07-145087-4)

An overview for first-time project managers that details what is expected of him or her and how to quickly get the lay of the land.

The Welch Way: 24 Lessons from the World's Greatest CEO
By Jeffrey A. Krames (0-07-138750-1)

Quickly learn some of the winning management practices that made Jack Welch one of the most successful CEOs ever.

The Lombardi Rules: 26 Lessons from Vince Lombardi–the World's Greatest Coach
By Vince Lombardi, Jr. (0-07-141108-9)

A quick course on the rules of leadership behind Coach Vince Lombardi and how anyone can use them to achieve extraordinary results.

Making Teams Work: 24 Lessons for Working Together Successfully
By Michael Maginn (0-07-143530-1)

Guidelines for molding individual team members into a solid, functioning group.

Managing in Times of Change: 24 Tools for Managers, Individuals, and Teams
By Michael Maginn (0-07-144911-6)

Straight talk and actionable advice on making sure that any manager, team, or individual moves through change successfully.

Persuasive Proposals and Presentations: 24 Lessons for Writing Winners
By Heather Pierce (0-07-145089-0)

A short, no-nonsense approach to writing proposals and presentations that sell.

The Sales Success Handbook: 20 Lessons to Open and Close Sales Now
By Linda Richardson (0-07-141636-6)

Learn how the consultative selling approach makes everyone in the transaction a winner. Close more sales and create long-term relationships with customers.

How to Plan and Execute Strategy: 24 Steps to Implement Any Corporate Strategy Successfully
By Wallace Stettinius, D. Robley Wood, Jr., Jacqueline L. Doyle, and John L. Colley, Jr. (0-07-145604-X)

Outlines a field-proven framework to design and implement a corporate strategy that strengthens an organization's competitive advantage.

The New Manager's Handbook: 24 Lessons for Mastering Your New Role
By Morey Stettner (0-07-141334-0)

Here are 24 quick, sensible, and easy-to-implement practices to help new managers succeed from day one.

Finance for Non-Financial Managers: 24 Lessons to Understand and Evaluate Financial Health

By Katherine Wagner (0-07-145090-4)

This guide offers a bundle of lessons to clearly explain financial issues in layman's terms.

Getting Organized at Work: 24 Lessons to Set Goals, Establish Priorities, and Manage Your Time

By Ken Zeigler (0-07-145779-8)

Supplies tips, tools, ideas, and strategies for becoming more organized with work tasks and priorities in order to get more done in less time.

The Handbook for Leaders: 24 Lessons for Extraordinary Leadership

By John H. Zenger and Joseph Folkman (0-07-143532-8)

A workplace-tested prescription for encouraging the behaviors and key drivers of effective leadership, from one of today's top training teams.

Outside the USA, order multiple copies of McGraw-Hill Professional Education titles from:

Asia

McGraw-Hill Education (Asia)
Customer Service Department
60 Tuas Basin Link, Singapore 638775
Tel: (65)6863 1580
Fax: (65) 6862 3354
Email: mghasia@mcgraw-hill.com

Australia & New Zealand

McGraw-Hill Australia Pty Ltd
82 Waterloo Road
North Ryde, NSW 2113, Australia
Tel: +61-2-9900-1800
Fax: +61-2-9878-8881
Email: CService_Sydney@mcgraw-hill.com

Canada

Special Sales Representative, Trade Division
McGraw-Hill Ryerson Limited
300 Water Street
Whitby, Ontario L1N 9B6
Tel: 1-800-565-5758

Europe, Middle East, Africa

McGraw-Hill Professional, EMEA
Shoppenhangers Road, Maidenhead
Berkshire SL6 2QL, United Kingdom
Tel: +44 (0)1628 502 975
Fax: +44 (0)1628 502 167
Email: emma_gibson@mcgraw-hill.com

Other Areas

For other markets outside of the U.S., e-mail Bonnie Chan at
bonnie_chan@mcgraw-hill.com.

Negotiate Your Way to Success
Order Form

1–99 copies	_____ copies @ $7.95 per book
100–499 copies	_____ copies @ $7.75 per book
500–999 copies	_____ copies @ $7.50 per book
1,000–2,499 copies	_____ copies @ $7.25 per book
2,500–4,999 copies	_____ copies @ $7.00 per book
5,000–9,999 copies	_____ copies @ $6.50 per book
10,000 or more copies	_____ copies @ $6.00 per book

Name _____

Title _____

Organization _____

Phone (____)_____

Street address _____

City/State (Country) _____ Zip _____

Fax (____)_____

Purchase order number (if applicable) _____

Applicable sales tax, shipping and handling will be added.

☐ VISA   ☐ MasterCard   ☐ American Express

Account number _____ Exp. date ____

Signature _____

Or call 1-800-842-3075
Corporate, Industry, & Government Sales

The McGraw-Hill Companies, Inc.
2 Penn Plaza
New York, NY 10121-2298